Glamorous ROOMS

Glamorous ROOMS

JAN SHOWERS

ABRAMS, NEW YORK

Contents

FOREWORD

by

MICHAEL KORS

I met Jan in the mid-1980s—ironic, since at that time design was at a low point. Fashion or interiors, it didn't matter, there was plenty of bad taste to go around. We were both in the earliest stages of our new careers when we first became acquainted, and we gravitated toward one another immediately.

Partly, the attraction was due to our mutual respect for each other's taste. I loved Jan's style, which was particularly American: restrained, smart, and always glamorous; she was never a fashion victim at a time when that was nearly impossible. She was a big fan of my work and wore my designs just the way I liked to envision them—with elegance and ease, but no fussiness. It was always a thrill to see her at my trunk shows because I knew that, if no one else did, she absolutely got it.

But it wasn't just fashion that brought us together. Naturally, we were concerned with the struggle of discovering where we fit into our respective worlds, while at the same time keeping an eye on the big picture. We didn't think of ourselves as *merely* a fashion designer or as *just* an interior decorator; we each felt that we were building careers in which, if we did everything right, we could really succeed. Fortunately, neither one of us had any idea then of how much tenacity, time, and good luck would be required to launch lasting careers, to say nothing of creating a lasting style. Back then, we simply shared an artistic aim: We were opposed to everything that was momentary and fleeting, and while we understood that our work should draw inspiration from the greats in our fields, we wanted to do work that no one else was doing.

The power of magazines, books, and films as inspiration cannot be overstated. My personal style reflects the influences of Jacqueline Kennedy Onassis in the 1970s, actress Catherine Deneuve in *Belle de jour*, the iconic styles of Grace Kelly in the 1950s, and the American socialite Babe Paley, pictured standing poolside at her Jamaican villa.

On film, the meticulous and creative art direction of Alfred Hitchcock astounds me still, and I return to those images time after time for inspiration. Hitchcock saves thirty minutes of exposition by showing the houses and rooms of his characters. In *To Catch a Thief*, Cary Grant's villa tells you all you need to know about his character, an understated, sophisticated man who enjoys life in his house and garden. Anthony Minghella's *The Talented Mr. Ripley* and *Plein Soleil*, René Clément's original adaptation of Patricia Highsmith's novel, are filled with costumes and interiors that I admire.

These collective influences reinforce the quality of timelessness. Timelessness is at the core of all my designs. It is the foundation of my work and of my design philosophy. The interior designer Billy Baldwin said, "Decorating is never successful unless it's personal." I agree wholeheartedly. No house should look like a hotel suite. I must know you before I can design your home.

One of my favorite design books is Dorothy Draper's charming *Decorating Is Fun!* I love this title, which itself captures a genuine belief of mine. Too often, I've heard complaints about the grueling ordeal of decorating a house. This should never be the case! Decorating should be wonderfully gratifying as you focus on surrounding yourself with things you love. And besides, decorating is not a small expense; you should enjoy the experience.

At first glance, the rooms I design might appear to be very simple. It is only after taking a closer look that one discovers the underlying complexity. Fine details are central to my interiors. They are the link to the story of a room and the people who live there. One's taste, interests, sense of humor, and history can be discerned through the details of a space, for those who care to see. The use of detail, and the knowledge of what to include where, is a skill I refer to as "the art of the mix." Thinking in unconventional terms; mixing styles, family traditions, eras, and textures; and learning to play with expectations is the way I create glamorous rooms.

Design, like life itself, should be full of surprises and happy accidents. I always believe the best results are achieved by remaining flexible and keeping an open mind.

Glamour is fundamental to all of my work. Though it's difficult to define, I can tell you without reservation what it is not. Glamour is not shiny satin and fox wraps from films of the 1930s. It is not a fad, and it is never over the top. When I think of glamour, I think of the strength of Katharine Hepburn in a black turtleneck and black pants with a red scarf thrown around her neck, or the exquisite unpretentiousness of Audrey Hepburn in Capri pants, ballet flats, and a white shirt.

Glamour is at the intersection of timelessness, simplicity, originality, and unqualified confidence in good taste. Glamour in design is just the same. Think of the fabulous Villa Fiorentina, which Billy Baldwin designed for Mary Wells and Harding Lawrence. It is the epitome of glamour and sophistication. In a locale and era in which many houses were designed in the formal French manner, Baldwin chose instead to draw inspiration from the blues of the water and sky, so plentiful in the south of France, filling the salon with luxuriously comfortable sofas and simple, flat-weave rugs. That room is understated and perfectly elegant.

Just as important as glamour is the concept of appropriateness. This is a notion that cannot be emphasized enough. It's dreadful when, for instance, over-the-top drapery is used in a small and otherwise modest cottage. I knew a woman whose bedroom had nine-foot ceilings, yet she insisted on having her bed done in the style of Marie Antoinette. That bed belongs only in Versailles. One should always ask, "Is it appropriate?" Billy Baldwin and Elsie de Wolfe used the word "suitability" to describe the same concept. If something is not suitable for the space, don't even consider using it.

Never forget that well-considered rooms represent a way of life. That fact is central to any project. When you design a room, do not think only of achieving high style. Comfort has to be a top priority. While stuffy, unwelcoming rooms may be beautiful in a photograph or when viewed through a window, they are, in reality, quite uncomfortable. Spaces should not only be inviting, but they should also encourage guests to linger.

I truly believe in these rooms as living works of art. That's more than just a high-minded ideal to me.

Jan Showers

Entry HALLS

I f every house tells a story, each entry hall is an opening chapter. And nothing makes you give up on a book faster than a boring introduction. Whether the message is intended or not, when you enter through the front door of a house, you learn something about the residents. A wonderful variety of styles and moods can be achieved in an entry. A relaxed hall in a country house makes a statement, as does an incredibly glamorous entry with mirrored walls, or a sleek modern hall featuring one stunning piece of art. You can fall in love with any of these spaces, from bold and exciting to casual and fun.

Perfection in design doesn't mean that there's one right way of doing things. An extraordinary truth about design is that the same space can be made perfect in any number of ways, depending on who is using it and what they want. There are absolutely no rules to creating the ideal environment other than this: Never be meek; always make a statement.

Silver-leaf tea paper creates a subtle yet glamorous impact on walls, where it serves as an ideal backdrop for mirrors, as well as mirrored or painted furniture. The glow of a beautiful lamp against the silver has an indescribably delicate and wonderful effect. When choosing between simple silver leaf—meaning an absence of gold undertones— and warm silver leaf, one should always opt for the latter. Standard silver leaf usually ends up appearing dimensionless and flat, a word that is highly undesirable when it comes to design—or anything else for that matter!

In entry halls, as in life, there is no greater offense than saying nothing at all. Make a statement. Stanley Barrows designed the elegant doors that access this alluring townhouse. The well-placed bench is the work of the American midcentury modernist Edward Wormley.

Since entries serve a purpose as passageways into the body of the house, they often come with their own unique set of design dilemmas. The entry of my own country house was a tremendous problem. An architecturally traditional three-story Georgian Revival, its interiors are nothing if not unexpected. The entry hall is the weakest architectural element of the house, and I struggled with its design. It is disproportionately small in relation to the rest of the house and has a staircase occupying almost one third of the available space along the left wall. To address the room's shortcomings, I placed a nineteenth-century painted and gilded console opposite the staircase. Above it, a wonderful antique mirror. A pair of stripped and carved pine lamps with box-spaced silk shades finishes the high-style concept of the space, which might otherwise serve as nothing but a pass-through were it not for these elements. That room tells all who enter, "This house will not be what you expected before you came inside."

Inordinately large entry halls often prove to be the most troubling, since it is difficult to arouse feelings of drama and intimacy in an overscaled room. One of the most successful large entry I have encountered is in a 1920s Beverly Hills Mediterranean-style house. Its strength is that it affords so many vistas and a stunning insight into the rest of the house. Standing in the middle of the entry hall, one can see the living room and the solarium just beyond; to the right, a dining room and gallery; and to the left, a staircase with an opening to a man's study on the landing. That space is successful because it is so inviting; guests always wish to explore each of these rooms.

Large entries like that one usually have high ceilings, which can be another barrier to creating a feeling of intimacy. The best solution in those spaces is the use of bold furniture and art hung at eye level, bringing the eye down and giving it a place to rest. When combined with chandeliers hung at a relatively low height, these pieces can counteract the effects of a voluminous space.

Whatever design challenges they may pose, bold choices pay tremendous dividends in entry halls. Take chances, and never, never allow these spaces to bore!

A painting by Tony Horton adds drama to an entry hall that features nineteenth-century Flemish chairs upholstered in unexpected white and black leather.

OPPOSITE, ABOVE, AND OVERLEAF: Create an aura of glamour with
some or all of these classic design elements: warm silver-leaf tea paper on
the walls, a fabulous Murano-glass lamp, gilded mirrors, a pair of eighteenth-
century painted Italian slipper chairs, and a graphic animal skin on the floor.

PREVIOUS: If the ceiling is ten feet or higher, find the perfect chandelier for your space, such as an ornate seventeenth-century painted wood Italian chandelier (left) or a 1920s French treasure (right) made of iron and glass. **OPPOSITE AND ABOVE:** Designing around a staircase can be a challenge. The best method for this architectural arrangement is to nestle a table, an exquisite pair of benches, or a set of chairs at the landing. With the addition of an elegant lamp, a vase of flowers, and a stack of books, a space of both intimacy and utility is created in the most public of your house's rooms. **OVERLEAF:** The needlepoint zebra chairs are all this entry needs for high drama.

If there is sufficient room for a commode or console in your entry, use a lamp or a pair of lamps. The warm glow at eye level is so lovely that visitors are drawn inside. **OVERLEAF:** Art creates its own lighting demands. This James Nares painting hangs in an entryway under the light of a 1950s Vistosi Murano chandelier. A sculptural lamp by Wily Daro is reflected in the lacquered commode and a bronze framed mirror designed by Maison Jansen.

Living
ROOMS

Living rooms should be comfortable and formal, suited both to private repose and lively gatherings. Typically, the greatest amount of funds for the interior design of a house is allocated to the living room. Yet, ironically, living rooms—which are too often reserved for formal occasions and large parties—can also be the one room of the house in which the family spends the least amount of time. Living rooms should be lived in—whether by groups of four or forty.

Visualize your family members gathered in the living room reading the morning paper, playing games, or listening to music in the late afternoon with the dogs sitting about on the floor in front of the fire. Maybe everyone is resting or conversing, or simply enjoying their morning coffee. This is what a truly successful living room should accomplish. Otherwise, why have one? Every room in your house should be a reflection of your life as you live it. Rooms should never exist as museum settings meant only to impress visitors. There is nothing worse than cushions that go untouched and pillows that are never moved from their places. What a depressing thought!

In practical terms, the success of this philosophy is dependent on making the living room into a place where people wish to spend time. Imagine ways to seduce and lure family and friends into using the neglected spaces, such as books stacked high on tabletops along with filled magazine racks, which never fail to make rooms appear more layered and welcoming.

Comfortable pillows add color and dimension to this Van Day Truex-style sofa
and stacked books on the gold-leaf Sabine coffee table invite guests to stay a while.

Louis XV–style bergères and vintage Murano lamps with
custom-designed yellow lampshades flank a 1960s tufted silk
sofa, proving that glamour can be accomplished with ease.

As a rule, it's best to use one large rug as opposed to several small ones, as it creates a grander and more gracious look, especially in this eclectic room with ebonized Dorothy Draper commodes; 1960s ceramic bamboo lamps; my Salon sofa; chairs with great character, including my "Louis XVII" chairs; and Louis XVI-style painted fauteuils upholstered in chocolate-brown leather.

Though technology is rarely the first thing on our minds, living rooms outfitted with a telephone and television are used more often than those without them. And why not? Shed outdated ideas about maintaining an excessively formal atmosphere in the living room. If the television is integrated into elegant bookcase beside the fireplace, one never notices its presence unless it's turned on—which is just as it should be. It is wonderful to relax there in front of a fire and have the choice to watch a great old movie or read a book.

What is a more inviting element than a living room fireplace? The sounds, smells, and warmth of a fireplace are unlike anything else in the world. They have the power to transform the mood of any setting. Shed the pressures of the day beside the glow of your own living room fireplace.

The selection of a wonderful rug is one of the most important decisions made early in the design process. Very often, people wish to use smaller rugs in order to show more of their wood or stone floors, but they are always pleased when they see the effect of a larger rug in the space. Rugs should be kept understated and elegant. Though it's not a hard-and-fast rule, low-contrast rugs typically work best. However, you may opt for a high-contrast black-and-white graphic rug to mitigate the vastness created by a double-height ceiling.

Anyone familiar with my interiors will notice vintage skins and cowhides used on the floors. While I'm not a big fan of wearing fur, I see skins as a fabulous addition to just about any room. Though some may object, I find that they create instant glamour. I also love to upholster furniture in white cowhide for the same reason. Obviously, I understand that this look isn't for everyone, and I certainly don't use animal skins to be controversial. One should certainly not support the trade of skins of any endangered animal, as that is never glamorous.

Coffee tables in my designs often have mirrored tops, like this Portofino coffee table. There is something magical about looking down on reflective surfaces. They reveal another dimension in every room and are perfect for the display of collections of glass.

After rug choices have been addressed, a decision can be made about the color of the walls. Do not use wallpaper in living rooms. The most beautiful walls are painted French boiserie, with its wonderful carvings and subtle depth. Or smooth plaster finishes, which have a rich and soft appearance. Or even heavily lacquered walls. Talk about dramatic! Many houses have neither boiserie, plaster, nor lacquered walls; rather, they have drywall. Drywall can be fine, but it is critical to understand that highly textured walls with repetitive patterns are an insurmountable barrier to good style. One should always insist on extremely smooth walls.

In selecting wall colors, the paints of Benjamin Moore, Donald Kaufman, Farrow & Ball, and Fine Paints of Europe are favored. The pigments they use in making their colors are quite different from the standard paints. Greens are a classic choice in public spaces, and they are a neutral, just as ivory is a color. Blues are soothing, and yellow, while too active a color for bedrooms, can be just right in a living room, where its cheeriness is desirable. By lamplight, it creates a wonderfully warm glow in the evening. Platinums and grays are underused. People tend to think of them as too cold, but that's not the case. They actually create an incredibly luxurious atmosphere. Deeper colors than these are better reserved for powder rooms, entry halls, libraries, and studies.

Since they are the largest spaces in the house, it is smart to divide living rooms into at least two seating areas, or three or four if the space allows. This creates intimacy. One area should be for conversation and gathering (usually around the fireplace) and another can be for more solitary tasks, perhaps a desk for writing notes or working on a computer. When possible, incorporate a game table for cards, puzzles, and projects.

Once the seating areas have been established, it's time to begin shopping for wonderfully comfortable sofas, chairs, and banquettes. Scale is the most important consideration here.

The character of a space is largely established by the history and age of the pieces it contains. In this room, a Napoleon III slipper chair from 1860 sits under a Stewart Cohen photograph. A Maison Jansen mirror hangs above my Hadley sofa.

While exercising particular care in considering the scale of your furniture, I recommend a more relaxed attitude about fabrics in general. Don't be too cautious or worried about fabric selections, fearing accidents and spills. These rooms should be designed for luxury. Nothing is more luxurious than being comfortable and enjoying one's environment. Mix textures and styles liberally. Cashmeres, low-sheen satins, linens, silks, velvets, mohair, and wonderfully ironed and waxed leathers are favored textures in living rooms. When possible, preserve original upholstery and leather. We should take a lesson from the British; they value aged fabrics, ones that look worn and lived in. Original leather especially should not be replaced if it can be saved. The softness and patina of aged leather is something that can never be reproduced. The Duchess of Windsor kept the same fabric in her Paris dressing room for many years. When it finally deteriorated and had to be replaced, she requested that the manufacturer of the new fabric (which was identical to the old fabric) place it in the sunlight to give it a slightly aged appearance.

Patterns other than stripes on upholstered pieces are not recommended, as they can become tiresome. Rely instead on pillows to bring color and pattern — as well as comfort — into a room. Geometric designs, color blocking, and pillows with embroidered detail also add interest and color. When used properly, pillows — along with flowers and great glass pieces and lamps — are truly the finishing touches in a glamorous room.

Once the larger elements are established, it's time to bring in "character chairs." That is, chairs that make a statement, such as a Louis XVI fauteuil, a Klismos-style chair, or a Mies van der Rohe Barcelona chair. Nothing will shape the look of a room more. Don't expect these chairs to be the most comfortable in the setting. They are very rarely fully upholstered. Rooms in which every single piece of furniture is fully upholstered are boring. Too much upholstery is one of the most prevalent mistakes made in present-day design, because it lacks detail and interest. Detail is critical to establishing the singularity and quality of any piece: the unique carving on the leg of a chair, the graceful sweep of the arm of a sofa, the style and quality of fine upholstery, the exquisite casting of a coffee table leg — all of these elements go into creating a polished room.

Rooms should be filled with things that make us feel vital and joyous, and nothing brings a sense of joy to a space the way that flowers can. I always keep orchids, one of my favorite flowers, in the living room on this vermeil, mirrored three-piece French coffee table.

Many furniture designers and manufacturers have shown progressively less attention to detail, contributing to the unfortunate trend of houses resembling generic hotel rooms, filled with bland, undetailed, and easily copied furniture. One should learn to recognize finely detailed, bench-made furniture and finishes that true artisans execute properly. Antiques should also be used in every room in a house, at least one per room. The character of a space is largely established by the history and age of the pieces it contains.

Every chair must have its own table, or one close by in the case of a coffee table or tea table. This is a necessity, as one must always have a place to lay a book or set a drink. In almost all cases, a lamp for reading should also be present.

Decorative glass, such as bowls, vases, and decanters, introduce color and shimmer to a space in a way that nothing else can. Each piece of glass creates its own unique luminosity. Throughout her life, my grandmother displayed her crystal and glass collections, so that glass pieces were spread throughout every room of her house. As a child wandering through the rooms of that house, my passion for glass was awakened. It was magical for me then and I'm still in love with it. I wish always to be surrounded by great collections of glass. Even today, when shopping for antiques, a wonderful piece of glass always attracts my eye and excites me.

When hand-painted papers are used on the walls, floors shouldn't compete. Parquet floors are a good option in these instances. If the walls are simply painted, imagine marble floors done in the French manner, with large square tiles and small diamond-shaped dots set at regular intervals. With sufficient veining the marble tiles should look old. Hone your marble floors so they appear softer. *Shiny* should be treated as an undesirable word when describing marble floors.

In thinking about the design of a room, people should keep in mind the things that really complement them. For example, when putting together a room, I find that many people give little thought to the colors and fabrics that suit them best, while these same people will agonize over clothing decisions that will affect them for a much shorter amount of time. You should look and feel as good in your favorite room as in your favorite outfit.

While pretty mirrored tables reflect the natural light in a room, lamps are truly the jewelry. Here a moonstone Venetian lamp stands on the Eliza table, offering great style even when switched off.

Nothing is more luxurious than being comfortable and enjoying one's environment. Mix textures and styles liberally. The nineteenth-century Venetian mirror reflects a midcentury turquoise Murano lamp and custom faux-skin coffee table, making for a luxuriously comfortable living room.

High style can be achieved in a living room such as this one—with a gold-leaf India table, Duchess mirror, and Palm Beach sofa—where comfort is still a top priority. The pops of turquoise add glamour and excitement.

ABOVE: It's the details that matter most. Behold a Dino Martens lamp with French twisted silk cord that's just as attractive as the lamp itself.
OPPOSITE: This living room encourages guests to linger in cozy French Art Deco chairs. **OVERLEAF:** These Maison Jansen vermeil lamps make a space feel fresh and au courant, and mixing silver and gold is always a good idea.

This living room exemplifies the art of mixing periods and styles. Here, an eighteenth-century French daybed and Napoleon III tufted slipper chairs divide the room into two seating areas. This creates intimacy, especially around the custom-designed mirrored mantel with Fontana Arte lamps.

OPPOSITE: Using a graphic rug causes one to focus more at eye level, which is what is needed in rooms with overly high ceilings. This Stark carpet complements the ivory lacquered wing chairs and mirrored floor lamp.

ABOVE: Detail is critical to establishing the singularity and quality of any piece: the unique carving on the leg of a chair, the graceful sweep of the arm of a sofa, the style and quality of fine upholstery, the exquisite casting of a coffee table leg—all of these elements go into creating a polished room.

ABOVE: A collection of nineteenth-century French *herbiers* line a hallway, hanging perfectly behind a forged iron table and a pair of 1930s ebonized Art Deco chairs. **OPPOSITE:** Vintage skins used on the floor are a fabulous addition to just about any room. They create instant glamour and sex appeal. **OVERLEAF:** A red lacquered Asian coffee table becomes the communal centerpiece under an amber Murano chandelier in this splendid living room. The art of this mix: a pair of gold-and-silver mercury glass lamps, an elegant pair of 1960s lounge chairs, and a pair of French 1940s slipper chairs upholstered in Hinson "Snow Leopard."

ABOVE: The warm glow of the hand-washed yellow-gold walls invites one to sit down and relax in this living room. Chairs, tables, and lamps are all from the 1940s. OVERLEAF: A pair of Murano vintage lamps balance a living room wall, with a Napoleon III gilded writing desk, well-placed artwork, a collection of vintage yellow Murano glass, and plaster artist model molds.

ABOVE: Another view of the yellow-gold room from the previous spreads, with the addition of robin's-egg-blue chairs for spring. OPPOSITE: The colors of nature can always be used as a neutral. This hand-blown Petal lamp is the color of the early summer sky; it sits on a mirrored dressing table and so the sparkle is doubled.

OPPOSITE: A nineteenth-century alabaster chandelier and a 1950s ceramic lamp illuminate this bold room. Thinking in unconventional terms; mixing styles, family traditions, eras, and textures; and learning to play with expectations is the way I create glamorous rooms. Note how the 1930s Art Deco chair covered in skin and the sofa covered in Rose Cummings toile sit comfortably together on a Stark Les Damiers rug. **ABOVE:** A simple but glamorous combination: a pairing of Napoleon III lounge chairs, a 1940s onyx and bronze coffee table, the Palm Beach banquette, and a pair of Capri floor lamps. **OVERLEAF:** Classic glamour: a custom sofa, vintage Murano lamps, an Empire settee in yellow satin, a Serena mineral lamp, and a 1960s bronze lacquered and mirrored vintage coffee table.

PREVIOUS: Trade secrets revealed: Clarence House zebra tapestry on a Palm Beach banquette and French 1940s ebonized fauteuils upholstered in trademark hairy hide surround a Maison Jansen coffee table. Hinson floor lamps and an antique coromandel Chinese screen make this room glamorous yet livable.

ABOVE: Every chair must have its own coffee table or tea table, or one close by. This is a necessity, as one must always have a place to lay a book or set a drink.

OPPOSITE: A mix of styles makes a modern townhouse as comfortable as a cottage: An Ellsworth Kelly drawing hangs above the Paris banquette, which features two Saarinen Tulip tables in front of it, and a René Drouot gilded iron coffee table sits on the Stark Ellipse rug.

PREVIOUS: In this formal living room, proportion is observed with a Swedish Empire-style chandelier. Scale was also carefully considered in the selection of the sofa, Jean Rothschild chairs, and nineteenth-century candelabra lamp by Baccarat.
ABOVE AND OPPOSITE: Never be afraid to mix patterns, periods, and wood finishes. Here, a Manuel Canovas stripe on the Rothschild chair ties all of the elements of this room together.

ABOVE: Both the fireplace and coffee tables are the focal points in this room, especially with the stunning painting by Hans Hoffman hanging above them. OPPOSITE: Rock crystal obelisks reflect beautifully on this Bagues three-piece bronze-and-mirrored coffee table from the 1950s. It is surrounded by Napoleon III tufted chairs and a pair of Maison Jansen gilded chairs from the 1940s.

PREVIOUS: This sunroom is splendid with comfortable upholstery fabric. Behold a Murano palm chandelier from the 1940s and the pair of floor lamps, as well as the French gilded-iron coffee table and Louis XV–style bergères in white cowhide. **ABOVE:** To create a more streamlined look, I used the Paris Banquette and a gilded-iron French 1940s coffee table. **OPPOSITE:** A bronze-and-marble table from the 1950s is placed next to a French 1940s Louis XV–style bergère upholstered in my signature white cowhide.

OPPOSITE: An unusual collection of Venetian glass from the 1940s and 1950s. **ABOVE:** This room is full of furnishings from my own furniture collection: the Danielle Tête-à-Tête, Como table, Leland drinks cart, Capri floor lamp, and Venetian Series #1 lamp.

OPPOSITE: A Robert Longo print hangs over a nineteenth-century marble mantel. The Maxime Old coffee table with vintage Murano glass is placed to the left of the fireplace. **ABOVE**: Another mix of styles and eras. A mohair sofa is placed over a black cowhide rug in this rouge lacquered room with bold details, including a 1970s bronze coffee table with reverse gold-leaf glass top, vintage barware, Greek key pillows with Greek key smoking set, and a fabulous photograph by Slim Aarons, *Monocled Miss*, from 1964.

ABOVE: Details matter, as in the combination of Lucite, mirror, and architectural bronze in the Harrison coffee table, which adds character and glamour to any room. **OPPOSITE:** Don Bodine line drawings hang beautifully over a custom corner banquette in platinum silk satin.

OPPOSITE: This gold-leaf Japanese screen painted in the Chinese manner is the perfect backdrop for a fine collection of gold Murano and Barovier glass. **ABOVE**: A collection of vintage and antique obelisks.

ABOVE AND OPPOSITE: Collections of glass make a sparkling
statement on tabletops.

OPPOSITE AND ABOVE: One of my favorite fabrics from Rose Cummings, "Calladium," covers this room. The details: a hand-forged French 1940s coffee table, Louis XV–style chairs upholstered in white cowhide, and a collection of French ceramic pieces mixed with yellow Murano glass.

Art is the centerpiece of this room: The painting hangs over a Salon sofa and is surrounded by vintage Hollywood Regency ceramic lamps, a pair of 1960s tufted bergères, and a stunning lacquered Asian coffee table.

ABOVE AND OPPOSITE: A collection of limited-edition Matisse drawings of women from 1942 is perfectly placed above a Jules Leleu cabinet and an Art Deco ceramic lamp. Light woods, ivory, and a pale Donald Kaufman sage green paint create a serene room—with lots of glass to add an element of glamour.

ABOVE: The Salon sofa, a pair of nineteenth-century Biedermeier chairs, and a marbleized mirrored coffee table stand in front of a custom bookcase designed to feature art. **OPPOSITE:** The Stella sofa in robin's egg blue, a Kyle Bunting cowhide rug, and a chiseled glass lamp create a setting that is truly a glamorous room.

OPPOSITE: The designs in my own home include the Palm Beach banquette, the Portofino coffee table, the Link lamp, and a screen in the Italian style hand-painted by my mother. **ABOVE**: A collection of vintage chartreuse glass.

Dining
ROOMS

Dining rooms should be luxurious spaces designed for the pursuit of pleasure —pleasure in enjoying wonderful food and pleasure in the company of those with whom we enjoy spending time. Guests no longer pay unexpected visits to our houses. Today, gatherings in the home—whether formal or informal—are usually centered on dining. In some cases, visitors will spend more time in the dining room than in any other room of the house. And, of course, the family will spend a tremendous amount of time there as well—all the more reason to insist on impeccable, approachable design.

Picture yourself sitting around your dining table with family members, laughing, proposing toasts, and sharing a holiday meal. Envision friends in a warm, lovely environment, engaged in lively debates and stimulating conversations. Imagine a cozy atmosphere where the pressures of a hectic day are forgotten; a place for people to recharge over a beautiful meal and an excellent bottle of wine.

Missteps in dining room design tend toward two equally unpleasant extremes: austerity and excess. This is largely due to the elements implicit in dining room design—a large table and many matching chairs with straight backs. It's true that such pieces pose certain obstacles, but there are ways of lessening their impact. The aim should be to make foundation pieces feel like an integrated part of the room, a goal that is never met by matching all the components. A wonderful look is achieved, for instance, by pairing a mahogany or Merisier dining table with chairs finished in ivory lacquer. There's no need to match tables and chairs. The same principle applies to the elements of any well-decorated room. This is the art of the mix, which is truly the art of great design.

Hand-painted silver tea paper by Gracie covers the walls of this dining room,
and an amber Murano chandelier hangs over the round table and French 1940s
Merisier chairs upholstered in ironed and polished leather.

A dining room's design is primarily dictated by the size and shape of the room. Round tables are perfect in square spaces. And, in fact, round tables in general are preferred to square ones. They're easier to set and to seat comfortably. The same is true for oval tables in rectangular spaces. Any time more than eight guests are seated at a table, conversation becomes difficult, so in very large dining rooms, use two round tables, a solution that works surprisingly well, in terms of both utility and aesthetics.

One shortcut to an atmosphere of warmth is the use of dining chairs with upholstered backs. At a rectangular or oval table, have the host and hostess chairs upholstered in a different fabric than the other chairs if they are a different style. Upholstered chairs create a more comfortable experience for guests, making the room that much more luxurious and pleasurable. One never wants guests to be eager to leave the table. Seating in dining rooms should be inviting enough to keep people engaged throughout a long meal, as well as during coffee and dessert.

Either a buffet or a console—preferably an antique—should be used in every dining room. Their usefulness cannot be overstated, and they add elegance and charm. Sometimes these pieces are the most beautiful and unique of all the house's furnishings. In my own dining room, I have a large ebonized buffet with rouge leather center doors and legs with gilded accents. It is utterly glamorous, and it is indisputably a work of art. Often the interiors of these pieces are almost as stunningly crafted as the exteriors, as is the case with mine, which is entirely lined with sycamore.

Consoles are a less heavy choice and work well in rooms in which storage is not a concern. In a wonderful dining room I recently completed, a console was selected, not only because there was already ample storage in the house, but also because of the stunning hand-painted wall covering, which I did not wish to obscure. The antique Louis XVI–style console is painted in a hue similar to that of the walls, creating the impression of a floating surface.

A Venini fume chandelier and candles light this gold-leaf Japanese screen painted in the Chinese manner, Louis XVI–style dining table, and French Ruhlmann-style chairs from the 1930s.

I also use pedestals to wonderful effect in dining rooms, where they can fill the emptiness of corners. Frequently, buffets, consoles, and pedestals afford the only places available for the display of accessories, which are essential in adding another dimension or layer to a dining room. Lamps, flowers, interesting ceramics, glass, china, crystal, sculpture, and barware can all look great on these surfaces.

Such amazing barware was designed and fabricated in the 1920s and '30s. It's ideal for adding a touch of whimsy to a dining room. Although I am not a proponent of over-serving, and I know not everyone drinks alcohol, I must confess a fascination with the Thin Man movies starring Myrna Loy and William Powell; they always had the most wonderful bar trays with barware from this period. When collected, these pieces take on a frivolous, playful quality appropriate for display, not just in dining rooms but in living areas as well. They also present an opportunity to mix old with new. A few years ago, I picked up a bottle opener in the shape of a bartender quite inexpensively at a department store. It fits perfectly with my collection of vintage jiggers, cocktail shakers, and swizzle sticks. Adding lightness and fun to every room is essential.

When completing an interior, one must never overlook lovely jars, lamps, bowls, compotes, and unusual figures in ceramic, which can be paired beautifully with great glass pieces and will work in any setting.

Two lighting elements are central to all my dining room designs: chandeliers and lamps. Frequently, people are surprised when I suggest that lamps be placed on buffets. They create a luscious glow in a room that can be quite challenging to illuminate.

Because chandeliers in dining rooms should hang lower than in other rooms, I've always considered them to be in the category of eye-level lighting, which is my favorite kind of light, complementing people and creating warmth. Paired with lamps placed on buffets and auxiliary servers, the diffused light of chandeliers creates an aura of intimacy conducive to fine dining and conversation. A great chandelier can be the star of a dining room. In fact, I hang mirrors in almost every dining room I design primarily because they reflect and multiply the impact of chandeliers.

A nineteenth-century Venetian mirror reflects this stunning dining room's chandelier and a dazzling collection of vintage gold Murano glass on the table. A French sycamore buffet provides a surface for more lighting appropriate for dining: a pair of my Venetian candlestick lamps.

Dimmer switches on chandeliers are a must, as bright, bare bulbs can cast a harsh light, which makes people look unattractive. Candlelight should always be added to the mix—nothing creates a more enchanting atmosphere. But I am adamant about two important rules regarding candles: they should never be scented in dining rooms, and they should always be either ivory or white. I never use colored candles anywhere in my designs.

Wonderful china, crystal, and linens add another dimension to the dining room. What is more stunning than glittering crystal wine glasses and crisp white linens? China, though it should complement the colors of the walls as well as the surface of the table, need not match the walls. I chose a delicious apple green design on white for my dining room to go with deep blue-green walls. White linens are my favorite in most dining rooms; however, ivory linens have a place when trying to bring a sense of softness to a table.

In dining rooms, guests will likely remain in the same place for a long period of time with an unchanged perspective, which means that dining room walls are terribly important. Be certain to have something interesting on the walls for each guest to view. It is an occasion to showcase art, sculpture, and beautiful antiques that guests will have an opportunity to savor. Or one might prefer beautiful wall coverings, such as hand-painted chinoiserie, which can have a stunning impact and add glamour to dining rooms.

Always be mindful that some guests will have views into other parts of the house. Those lines of sight should be considered when formulating designs for adjoining spaces. The same is true of windows. Views of the outdoors can present either a grand opportunity or a terrible misstep. If your guests can see outside, be sure that they have a lovely view. The pleasure of enjoying a beautiful space can evaporate after looking onto an unkempt terrace or anything that is unsightly. It's ideal when dining rooms look onto outdoor rooms that have as much style as their indoor counterparts.

OPPOSITE AND OVERLEAF: A vintage Lucite bar cart with a personal collection of barware stands by my dining room, painted in Wythe blue.

As with formal living areas, I love the thought of utilizing formal dining rooms for ordinary meals and not reserving them just for special occasions. That said, I know that, in the modern house, casual dining spaces are used more frequently than formal ones. As far as I'm concerned, the same guidelines apply in these rooms as in more formal dining settings. Casual dining should be surrounded with beautiful objects and good lighting.

The wonderful advantage of alternate dining areas is the intimacy that comes with smaller rooms and tables. In my country house, I have two casual dining spaces. One is an antique glass-top garden table in my sunroom, positioned in front of a window with a view overlooking the garden and pool beyond. It is a favorite spot among friends and family. The other is a breakfast area near the kitchen, furnished with painted French garden furniture and benefiting from the morning light. I adore these spaces, which can be delightful for very informal meals, but can easily be transformed into cozy romantic settings. With the proper treatment, either of those spaces can rival my dining room as the ideal setting for a great meal. I also have a game table in our library that can be placed in front of the fireplace for two to four people.

In truth, any place can be a dining room—I'm in favor of having a table in almost every room of the house on which to dine.

An ebonized wood and crystal server from the 1950s displays a collection of nineteenth-century Limoges china in a dining room. A 1940s French fauteuil in the style of Andre Arbus adds curves to the room.

OPPOSITE: Classic glamour: A 1940s French dining table is
surrounded by Louis XVI-style dining chairs upholstered in their
original leather. The Barovier chandelier was designed by Andre
Arbus and the mirror is Venetian from the 1940s. Plaster *torchieres*
add dramatic light to the room. **ABOVE**: An unusual collection of
signed Jean Roget pottery.

A honey-colored Murano chandelier from the 1920s provides enough light for a work of art.

This collection of Matisse drawings is intimately lit by a Venetian glass lamp.

OPPOSITE: A Murano chandelier is reflected in a nineteenth-century gesso mirror. The lightness of the walls, drapery, floors, and upholstery highlight the lines of the dining table and chairs. **ABOVE:** The Loop dining chair is one of my favorite designs.

A pair of Serena lamps surrounds a collection of photographs above a
credenza by Jacques Adnet from the 1940s.

A mirror from the 1940s hangs across from a charming Murano chandelier from the same period with painted Klismos-style dining room chairs from the 1920s.

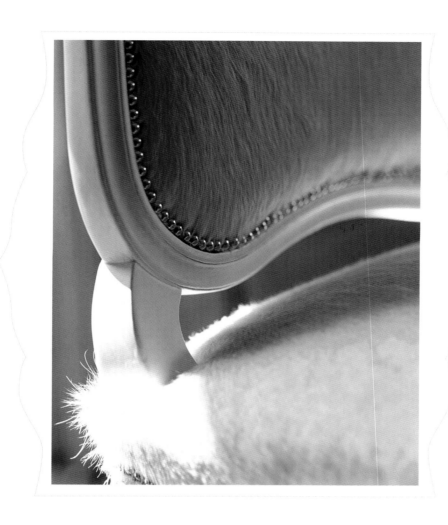

OPPOSITE AND ABOVE: My Antibes chair was upholstered in bittersweet-chocolate leather, and my Marnie chair in white cowhide was inspired by a Maison Jansen chair. **OVERLEAF:** A pair of glass rod lamps with mirror-and-bronze bases from the 1940s stand on a Louis XVI–style painted console with marble top and Greek key motif. A pair of frosted Venini chandeliers hang over this custom mahogany dining table with bronze details. Below it lies a gorgeous custom designed, hand-knotted Patterson, Flynn & Martin wool rug. The hand-painted wall covering is from Fromental.

ABOVE: My Marnie chairs surround a French Louis XVI–style table. OPPOSITE: French Louis XVI–style chairs—in hand-tooled robin's-egg-blue leather—are gathered around this eighteenth-century Louis XVI table. A Murano opaline chandelier from the 1920s and a pair of nineteenth-century French bronze *torchieres* light the room.

ABOVE: Verner Panton's shell chandelier adds an interesting element to this semiformal dining area with a French Louis XVI–style dining table, Louis XV–style painted dining chairs, and a French buffet from the 1950s. **OPPOSITE:** This informal dining area, with my Lombard table and Louis XVI-style chairs, is perfect for small dinner parties or for dining à deux.

OPPOSITE: All the furnishings in this room are in the Louis XVI style, from the 1940s, with the exception of the late-eighteenth-century mirror, a nineteenth-century Oushak rug, and a pair of amber Murano lamps from 1940.
ABOVE: A pair of gold Murano lamps stand on either side of a romantic nineteenth-century landscape, which hangs over a hand-painted French buffet.

Natural light and a yellow crystal chandelier light up this casual dining room with a French garden table and chairs by Raymond Subes from the 1940s. A light and lovely collection of classic English creamware fills the corner niches. Note the robin's-egg-blue ceiling—one of my favorite touches.

Bed
ROOMS

The bedroom should be the most luxurious room in the house. It is our true sanctuary, whether retiring after a long day, taking an afternoon nap, or waking on a weekend morning to read the newspaper and take coffee in bed.

Wonderful fabrics that evoke the feeling of being ensconced in a cocoon are a critical first step in building a sumptuous bed. That isn't to say that I advocate highly feminine beds. Quite the contrary, my preferences lean toward refinement and polish, in the spirit of David Hicks, the great English decorator, whose work has always been an inspiration to me. The beds I design feel as though they are rooms within the larger room. It is important to create a feeling of seclusion, as beds are often our only true retreats.

Bed hangings are my favorite approach in master bedrooms. They make the bed look important, which is exactly as it should be. Men are sometimes resistant to them, fearing that bed hangings will create an appearance of femininity, but, once convinced, they are always pleased with the results. Success is dependent on making everything look tailored and never fussy.

Coverlets, sometimes called blanket covers, are necessary. On top of coverlets, a plush duvet or, when working toward cleaner lines, an alpaca or cashmere blanket is great at the foot of the bed. Beds offer the ultimate opportunity for layering and mixing textures. Opposites work best. The best qualities of silks and satins are emphasized when paired with textured or low-sheen fabrics.

Absurdly puffy duvets that look to be over a foot deep are not luxurious; they are simply flamboyant and must be avoided. Obviously, if one is spending the night in the Swiss Alps in mid-winter, different rules might apply, but, generally, one should be able to sit on the bed without a feeling of sinking in quicksand. Ostentation is never a substitute for true comfort and fine taste.

This glorious custom bed treatment was inspired by the style of David Hicks. The Mercer bench is my own design.

Beds should envelop, feel warm and cozy, and have the best linens one can afford. I am always astounded when people are reluctant to buy good linens, yet are happy to spend much more on items that will impact their lives far less. Clearly, they have no idea what they are missing. Nothing should feel better than settling into your own bed!

It's lovely to use one or two hand-embroidered or colorful pillows as accents, although decorative pillows, like duvets, can be taken too far. Using too many creates an outdated look, as well as an obstacle when getting into bed. In this case, the "less is more" adage couldn't be truer. This is especially so when bed hangings are present.

Matching commodes are frequently employed as night tables in my designs, particularly in master bedrooms, where they provide additional storage and a generous surface for lamps, books, clocks, remote controls, and personal items. The appearance of commodes has the added benefit of lending solidity and symmetry around beds that can appear heavy when paired with lighter tables. So, for the sake of balance, I often use them even when storage is not a concern.

Bedrooms must have adequate lighting for reading. If there are bed hangings present, swing-arm pharmacy lights can be used, as the lamps on the tables next to the bed may be obscured by the side drapery.

The opulence of bedrooms should extend to the walls themselves. Soothing colors such as a soft greens and French blues are just right. Ivories and pale peaches complement skin tones, which is a very good idea in the bedroom. The most important thing, along with cultivating a relaxing environment, is creating one in which its occupants look their best. It's never a good idea to paint bedrooms red, and very seldom does yellow work either. These wonderful colors are too active for bedrooms. I once painted a bedroom of my own a deep Chinese red, and it was a disastrous mistake! It was practically impossible to get a restful night's sleep in that room. It was quickly repainted a soothing green.

When there is a preference for a monochromatic look in the bedroom, I introduce wall coverings, such as silks and grass cloths. They bring texture to a space and cultivate a feeling of lushness and abundance, with the added benefit of soundproofing.

The custom bed hanging accommodates the bookcases that line all the walls of this room. The Spencer bench is my own design.

L ike fabric-covered walls, carpet also serves as great sound insulation in the room where it matters most. I opt for either very large rugs or wall-to-wall carpeting in bedrooms. Wall-to-wall might be considered passé in some settings, but it lends to any bedroom a feeling of intimacy and warmth. As a rule, light-colored carpets look best.

Shades or blinds, no matter how handsome, never achieve the same lavish quality as drapery. My bedroom windows always have curtains.

In many instances, depending on your needs, there may be a dressing table or a desk in the bedroom, as well as a seating area, when there is sufficient room. Mirrored dressing tables are ideal.

A bench at the end of the bed are a must if the bed doesn't have a footboard. Benches of any size are items that I am always pleased to find when shopping. I favor them for their versatility and practicality. They are also perfect in entry halls and in front of fireplaces.

One rule I have when designing a house from the ground up is to avoid excessively large bedrooms. They simply never have the right feeling, no matter the scale of the furniture. I once had the challenge of redecorating a bedroom that was entirely too large. There was enough room for three seating areas, in addition to the bed and night tables. One or even two living spaces are fine, but three were entirely too many. The answer in that case was to increase the scale of each piece of furniture, but that is never an ideal solution, as I truly detest furniture that looks as if it is on steroids! Bedrooms that are too large will never achieve a feeling of intimacy. Also, I am not fond of bedrooms —or any rooms for that matter—with ceilings that are too high. The ideal height for a ceiling is ten to twelve feet.

I happen to have a small bedroom in my townhouse, with ten-foot ceilings and floor-to-ceiling windows. Because of the height of the ceiling I was able to have a bed with a flat canopy and curtains all around. It is the most wonderful bed I've ever slept in. The rest of the room is furnished with night tables, a chair, a small mirrored dressing table, and a table in front of a window with a television and lamp, and one grand mirror that is hung between two doors. It is one of the prettiest bedrooms I've ever seen, though relatively small.

More than any other room in a well-designed house, the master bedroom should reflect the spirit of its owner.

OPPOSITE: The Sarah bench, upholstered in white hairy hide with a gold-leaf base, looks understated and elegant placed at the end of a bed. OVERLEAF: A collection of antique perfume bottles (left) on a 1930s Lucite/mirrored tray in a dressing room, and Venini lamps circa 1925 (right) sit on a Maison Jansen Eglomise dressing table.

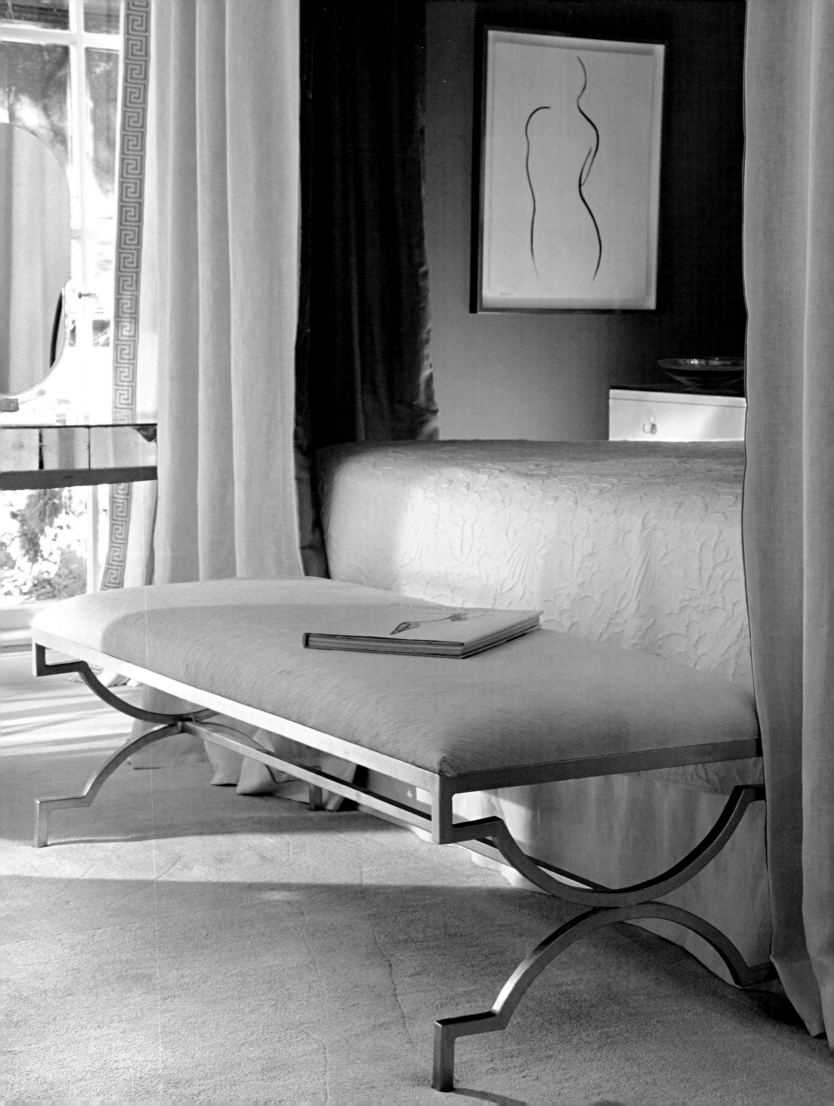

ABOVE: A sectioned mirrored screen adds depth and glamour to this bedroom.

OPPOSITE: A nineteenth-century Venetian mirror over the bed is reflected in another Italian mirror over the mirrored dressing table.

This custom Billy Haines—style bed in warm silver leaf is balanced by a pair of ivory lacquered commodes with white ceramic lamps and gold-leaf wood soleil mirrors from the 1940s.

OPPOSITE: The bed is your castle. This one includes Italian voile bed hangings, a Louis XV–style bench, and French blue silk duvet and pillows.
ABOVE: This bedroom with a fireplace is painted in a light blue. The details include the Pauline fire screen, Jules Leleu white-leather chairs, and a stunning Murano palm chandelier.

ABOVE: A pale Palladian blue room for a young woman, which includes a lovely pair of Claudette benches covered in Hinson "Snow Leopard," a French Directiore-style chandelier, and a soleil gilded mirror over the bed. **OPPOSITE:** Lighting was key in this room, with its dry-glazed walls in a French blue. Notice the French Art Deco bronze-and-glass chandelier and twisted gold Murano lamps. **OVERLEAF:** This Asian-influenced bedroom features a French Merisier commode with a Murano opaline lamp and a pair of turquoise Murano lamps.

PREVIOUS: A bed for a debutante with a custom bed treatment, including custom linens and French slipper chairs in the style of Andre Arbus from the 1940s.
ABOVE: This custom bed treatment includes a mix of linen, silk, and suede textures.
OPPOSITE AND OVERLEAF: The Manhattan side table is filled with all of my favorite things, most especially books.

PREVIOUS: Wickham Gray Benjamin Moore paint on the walls called for a custom bed treatment and custom linens, as well as a wonderful pair of Venini latticino Murano lamps and art by Rusty Scruby. **ABOVE AND OPPOSITE:** On this table: a 1920s alabaster "flame" lamp and an amber Murano-glass bowl. Don Bodine line drawings are framed on the French blue walls. A blue rug and coverlet, as well as a Claudette bench of my own design, bring this room together.

Groupings of miniatures, obelisks, shells, articles associated with a certain relative or locale—these are great examples of collections that make a house personal. I am not fond of collections displayed in vitrines. They remind me of old musty houses filled with clutter. Collections and personal items should be displayed artfully, whether on a tray or a special table.

Books should appear in every room, on shelves and tables, even stacked on the floor. I encourage everyone I know to visit vintage bookstores to find beautiful books that are out of print, particularly if they are interested in design, photography, and art. Nothing adds character to a room as much as books. There is nothing like a book to truly reflect your passions.

Even when used in the most modest of private spaces, such as by a simple chaise longue in the corner of a bedroom, books arranged in an interesting stack on the floor or on a nearby table create visual interest and a source of pleasure for whomever sits there. Obviously, in no room are books more at home than in libraries, where a wall of books becomes a wall of art. Bookcases that go straight to the floor are best for creating this effect. For an added touch of interest, framed art may be hung from the shelves of large built-in bookcases in the European style.

People often assume they don't have enough space for a private area if they don't have an individual room to dedicate to the purpose. I find that, when it is made a priority, the perfect space usually reveals itself. Maybe it's a corner in a living room where a desk can be used for writing notes, or perhaps it is a dressing area in one's bathroom, or a comfortable chair with a lamp nearby that lends itself to reading and private contemplation.

For some, a large closet is an ideal private space. It goes without saying that many women are collectors of beautiful clothes, handbags, jewelry, and accessories. I certainly consider the closet in my townhouse a private space. The same is true of the dressing room in my country house. It is painted in a soft yellow gold with draperies of ivory and gold toile de Jouy, one of the few patterns I love. I have furnished that room with a dressing table and desk, as well as a daybed, lounge chair, and ottoman. There, I am able to write letters, take a nap, get dressed for dinner, read, speak with friends on the telephone, work on my computer, or simply have quiet time alone.

A pair of fauteuils in their original faux leopard fabric, circa 1940, flank a coffee table with hooved feet and a Portoro marble top. The carpet is by Stark.

PREVIOUS: Not business as usual: late 1930s ebonized chairs sit in front of an eglomise reproduction mirrored desk with a Lucite and sycamore lamp. OPPOSITE: A vintage Murano blue lamp, Greek key eglomise picture frame, and a decanter on a 1930s French mirrored tray. ABOVE: A collection of Eiffel Towers on the Plaza desk in my office, along with the Lemon Drop lamp. I love to hang art from bookshelves in the European manner.

ABOVE: A dressing table skirted in harlequin-patterned silk; the center inverted pleat opens to reveal shelving. A large mirrored tabletop holds a perfume bottle collection. Classic French 1940s shield sconces flank a gessoed mirror. **OPPOSITE:** A 1940s Merisier desk in the Louis XVI style with a 1940s chair upholstered in Hinson's "Snow Leopard." The drapery fabric is hand-screened from Raoul Textiles.

Another French 1940s moment: a mirrored dressing table, scalloped mirror, and a Lucite bench.

A Napoleon III slipper chair with Greek key trim and a 1930s alabaster French floor lamp.

A dressing table from the 1940s, found in the south of France. Rose Cummings silk velvet adds a luxurious texture.

The Gigi chair in sycamore and ivory mohair provides a lovely spot for reading.

OPPOSITE: A bay window in a country house becomes the perfect place to relax. Here, the Caroline chair, upholstered in a sunny yellow linen, and the Mercer bench provide a lovely spot for conversation. **ABOVE:** A dressing room with a 1930s mirrored coffee table and a full-length 1920s French gilded mirror.

PREVIOUS: This sitting room in a young lady's high-rise features an Andre Arbus–style slipper chair and an etched mirrored coffee table. **ABOVE:** A collection of antique parchment books and ivory crackle bookends. **OPPOSITE:** A private space in the corner of a room with sycamore walls. The Villa sofa, the 1950s parchment coffee table, and Louis XVI–style fauteuils upholstered in chocolate-brown leather provide luxurious comfort.

Outdoor
LIVING

Some of my best memories are of dining on the terrace of my house in the country. That terrace has been the site of family gatherings, relaxed dinners with friends, and romantic evenings with my husband. I love being outdoors whenever possible. In modern life, our outdoor spaces are often the closest we come to nature. There is so much to enjoy outside: birds, trees, fireflies, fresh air, sunsets, and the stars at night. There is even the view into one's own home. In one of my favorite films, *Howards End*, Vanessa Redgrave walks the perimeter of her beloved house, peering through the windows and recalling scenes from her life there. I've done the same thing often at my own country house. One of the best things about an outdoor room can be the unique perspective it offers into the corresponding life indoors.

At our townhouse, in a much more urban setting, we have a lovely enclosed courtyard with trees and flowers, where we can interact with the outdoors and follow the changing of the seasons. That space is a great example of using an outdoor area as an extension of an interior space. I make sure on terraces and patios like this that the walls are painted in a hue similar to the interior color. The same is true of the floors, which are best when they match in tone, emphasizing the connection between indoors and outdoors. After all, your outdoor spaces should feel like any other room in your house—with equal attention paid to detail and style.

One of my favorite outdoor rooms is created by a border of hedges and a very simple floor of stone tiles set into the earth. Teak chairs and garden benches, along with iron-and-glass tables, sit out in the open, protected by only the branches of towering pecan trees. Nearby, a birdfeeder and birdbath. It is a picture of simplicity and comfort, and it serves perfectly as a vantage point from which to experience the outdoors, either alone or with others.

French-style garden furniture in a city courtyard, with glass lamps
for parties, is reflected in a custom convex mirror.

If an outdoor space is not bound by walls or a hedge, a "room" can be created by the addition of an awning or arbor. Sometimes an outdoor space can be grounded by something as simple as a rug. There are many good-looking outdoor sisals, or you could move an indoor rug outdoors for special occasions, as the French have done for centuries.

Of course, I wish for all the same comforts that I enjoy indoors to be outdoors as well. Successful outdoor spaces bring the indoors out. One must have a wonderful place for morning coffee and reading the newspaper, taking into consideration both shade and sunlight. I always use lamps in outdoor spaces, which are useful in early morning and evenings. Either table lamps or floor lamps work in protected areas such as loggias or under awnings.

The same building blocks must be used outdoors as in: sofas, coffee tables, lounge chairs, ottomans, lamp tables, dining tables, and chairs. As is my style indoors, I often mix new outdoor furnishings with antiques. Very often on buying trips, I find French iron garden furniture from the 1940s. Nothing like it has been made since, and it blends perfectly with sophisticated pieces from any era. I seldom have them repainted. The original finish is usually the most charming.

Outdoor furnishings with cushions should be at least partially protected from the elements. That said, the tremendous array of wonderful and durable outdoor fabrics is so chic and sophisticated that I often use them indoors.

Outdoor spaces without accessories always feel incomplete to me. When in use, my outdoor rooms include glass and ceramics, trays, flowers, palms, pillows, and even magazines—the best of everything like any other glamorous room.

The color of the plaster in this pool is reminiscent of the waters of the
Caribbean. Plaster lamps and sconces in the cabana evoke the south of France.

ABOVE AND OPPOSITE: Lush landscaping softens outdoor living spaces, and architectural elements add character and definition to large expanses.

OPPOSITE: From the indoors out: plaster lamps from the Eden Roc hotel, Sutherland teak with Perennials striped fabric, a metal mirror, and a French iron chandelier. ABOVE: Topiaries line the walls of this veranda to create a cool yet formal feeling. OVERLEAF: This loggia is cozy and inviting all year long, with its mix of modern outdoor furniture and vintage tables.

PREVIOUS: The shaded terrace of this Georgian Revival house is relaxed yet elegant. It features my favorite 1940s French garden furniture, upholstered in a crisp white outdoor fabric. **OPPOSITE**: Wallace Neff–inspired sofa and chairs, along with ceramic lamps and accessories, create a wonderful ambience in this Mediterranean-style loggia. More than any other element, lamps used in outdoor spaces create the feeling of a complete room. **PAGE 204**: The Desmond coffee table is an example of great form and finish in a room setting. Here, the table is seen in front of the Clarence House mohair sofa. **PAGE 206**: My Villa sofa, Harrison coffee table, Edie table, and Peony lamp make a soft statement on an unusually colored Oushak rug.

THE ART OF RICHARD TUTTLE

TWENTIETH-CENTURY
DECORATION
STEPHEN CALLOWAY

Michael S. Smith Elements of Style

JOHN RAWLINGS 30 Years in Vogue

CÉZANNE by himself   Kendall

Acknowledgments

I would like to sincerely thank the following people for their contributions to *Glamorous Rooms*.

Drew Smith for the hours spent talking to me about each and every image in the book—then taking my words and making them into exactly what I wanted them to be. Michael Kors, who has been a friend and inspiration for 25 years, for writing the wonderful introduction to Glamorous Rooms. Eva Prinz, my editor at Abrams, for believing in my work and having a vision of exactly how the book should look from the very beginning. Esther de Hollander for her constant support and guidance through this entire project. And to Kwasi Osei and Michelle Ishay-Cohen for their elegant design.

To all of the wonderful clients who have given me the opportunity to do the work that I love and allowed me to photograph their houses. Hinson & Company for their "Snow Leopard" fabric, which inspired the case for this book, and to Gracie for their warm silver-leaf paper, which was used to create the end sheets—both the fabric and the paper have served as beautiful additions to many of my interiors, and I am so pleased to have them be part of this book. The incredibly talented photographers who captured the rooms and detail shots, with a special thanks to Jeff McNamara. Meg Popejoy, my assistant and friend, who worked tirelessly to make sure that everything was done in a timely manner. And to the editors of all the major shelter publications who have published my projects over the past 20 years.

Most of all, I would like to thank my husband, Jim, who has encouraged and supported me in all of my endeavors, and who always believes that I can do anything.

EDITOR: EVA PRINZ
PROJECT MANAGER: ESTHER DE HOLLANDER
ART DIRECTOR: MICHELLE ISHAY
DESIGNER: KWASI OSEI
PRODUCTION MANAGER: JACQUIE POIRIER

Library of Congress Cataloging-in-Publication Data

Showers, Jan.
Glamorous rooms / by Jan Showers.
p. cm.
ISBN 978-0-8109-4974-4 (harry n. abrams, inc.)
1. Showers, Jan—Themes, motives. 2. Interior decoration—United States.
I. Title.

NK2004.3.S56A4 2009
747—dc22
2008049504

Printed and bound in China
10 9 8 7 6 5 4 3

Abrams books are available at special discounts when purchased in quantity for premiums
and promotions as well as fundraising or educational use. Special editions can also be created
to specification. For details, contact specialmarkets@abramsbooks.com or the address below.

THE ART OF BOOKS SINCE 1949
115 West 18th Street
New York, NY 10011
www.abramsbooks.com